On Eventide's Coattails

A Collection of Poetry

T.U. Patir

On Eventide's Coattails: A Collection of Poetry

All rights reserved. No part of this publication may be reproduced, scanned, or distributed in any printed or electronic form without prior permission. All opinions expressed in this book are the author's own. Thank you.

Copyright © 2024, Words, Cover and Photography by T.U. Patir
Self-Published by: Tridip Patir (aka T.U. Patir), 2024.
 Copyright © 2024, Art by Jahnvi Borgohain
Find more art on pinterest: jahnvisartdump

For more information, contact the publisher at:
tridippatir99@gmail.com

All rights reserved.

ISBN (Paperback Edition): 978-93-341-6114-4

To my dear mother, who has been a pillar for me. To Leo, for being the best dog ever, sorry I have not been there for you as much as I ought to. To my Cherry-Chipmunk, for you have been my light. You know who you are.

Finally, to 'evening', for this book would not exist were it not for you, and it is right that I dedicate its existence entirely to your magic. Without you, there is no me.

Preface

The poems collected in this bundle have been written over the course of a few years. Written on sleepless nights, about loneliness, sadness, loss, love, and even hope. The thoughts that roam our mind before sleep.

Riding on someone's coattails indicate that all your success has been because of the said person, i.e., you ride on their success.

To say, "On Eventide's Coattails" is to say that without eventide, or the evening, I would have reached nowhere. The evening time is when all emotions come flooding in, leading to all the poetry on display in this collection.

I have done nothing but capitalise on the romanticism of evening, its flaws and boons, alike. I, therefore, owe this book to none but the tides of the 'evening'.

Contents

Becoming 23

Acknowledgements

I thank all my mentors that I have had in various forms and in various fields, over the course of my currently young life. Thank You.

2

Was

Friends. friends, come go
But you, you stay
Why cry about what **was**?
When you can smile about what is?
Be happy with the number: one!

There, you can be whatever you desire to be.
You are playing the lead of your own movie, man.
How fun!

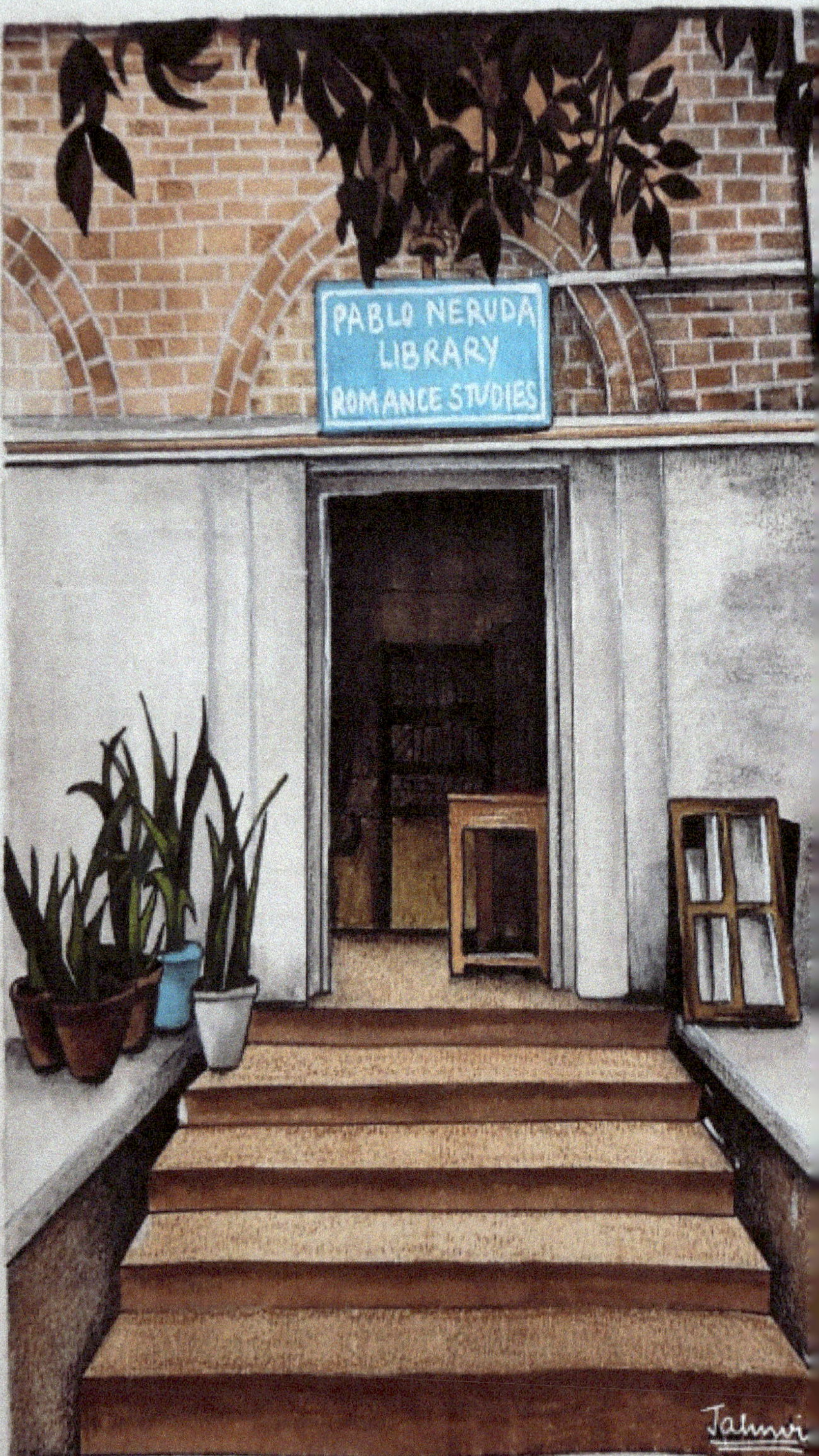
PABLO NERUDA
LIBRARY
ROMANCE STUDIES
Jahnvi

A Dream of a Dream

In dreams I thrive, with passions unbound,
Through a hundred miles along Featherbow Sound.
In between our hopes of multicoloured prism,
and with a twist of the eternal rain ever flooding a
grassy meadow.
You, me and our future packed in transparent
tupperware.

In dreams I thrive, in dreams I fly
And due nightfall?

I

shall

come

alive.

Here's to our dreams, then.
Till we part, on a day that never comes.

Mysterious Seamstress

Mysterious seamstress, you look to me
as though your eyes can see through my veil of
eluding
Illusive and magnetic, fields of platinum and gold.

You entered my dreams under the silent
moonbeam of springtime dust
And have made it evergreen.

Entwined

Much has been said of the nightly dreams,
That the sandman comes and gifts us all.
But the truest gift is life ever awaking,
A life to fight for and keep close at hand,
In truest form, in purest shine,
Your hand in mine,

Entwined.

Chance Meeting on Gaia

At a time of stillness in life ever-loving,
Took a minute to reflect on everything that has been
giving
From the dawn of my consciousness to this very
moment of understanding
You have been here, and I have seldom appreciated
you.

So, in the expanse of natural history,
From the minutest of organisms,
to the daunting size of exoworlds.
How fortunate, we humble hands,
To have a chance meeting on Gaia.

All of my breaths encompassing,
my soul everlasting, has led me to this moment,
Where I feel the warm embrace of your company,
And such company, can never be replaced.
Not replaced by golds or silver or the promise of
heavenly respite.

And despite, the thirst for salvation remains high
I would not trade that in a thousand of my
lifetimes for your pure laughter and your warm
smile.
If it be in my hands, I would freeze our moments
and spend every waking minute looking at your
face, beloved.
Until the frozen hours of time crumble and fade
away into naught,
and thus, there would be no more death, no more
passing,
And I would have you here with me, forever near,
forever lovely.

What amazing luck to be born in the same era as you,
And to have met so wildly,
 To feel the pain that has long troubled your soul
dissipating
And yet feel a tinge of sadness colour your palette
For when the angels would weep at your inevitable
parting

This lucky meeting takes many forms throughout life
And again and again, we hope it remains
"In all of my thousand lifetimes, I hope to remain..."

"Your mother"
"Your father"
"Your friend"
"Your beloved"
"Your soul"
"Your fire"

Ah...what amazing luck we've had
To have you near me, to hold you close with my
humble peasant hands
So, my beloved and my fire, consider this my heart laid
out open,
To thank you for this chance meeting on Gaia.

Reverie

Time runs short,
In this life, in this moment between the
blooming of a flower and the death of
spring.

Towards infinity, with outreached hands
mended by your mercy.
But too many flickers and transience in
this life.

I have so little time.
So, I rest my breath now,
But only for a moment.
For I have so much to say,
So much...

Tomorrow will never come

And despite your face lighting up each passing second
of my day,
 I can't help but be stuck with a notion,
Something pulls us, and then pushes us, and back again.
                The moon can relate, I am sure.

If I were born under a bad moon, I would want to be
reborn as a dove
Fly high through the trees and be loved by all.
 I have that dove in the form of you,
Your radiant light conquers the dusty blackness.
And yet I succumb.

If I were not meant to be here,
Why have I learnt to feel for the little
ones that roam hungry?
What is good?
What is the one true solution to end all
misery?
I digress...
I want to be the dove, or better, I want
to have the dove
 I then, have the dove,
but still, I sleep on a bed of stones

Either I have crossed into a foreign
country that speaks no tongues from my
yesteryears
Or you have moved back to your native
land forgetting the tongue that we used
to converse in.
 I guess it happens.

Empty shelves now dot my house.
They did once occupy your thoughts
Yes, you are here
But I need you to find me.
I hope you do someday.

Why are people so lonely?
Well, if I had somebody to talk to,
perhaps I could tell you.
I'll try again tomorrow.

Sarajevo by Candlelight

The shattered windows of a dingy apartment,
And Mrs Doe plays the cello despite the steady
burn.
She loses her world gradually
and she still smiles, the incumbent saviour.

I look around to see tiny children playing,
yanking around a stuffed horse.
Sweaters in the December cold.
The yanked horse is torn and can't run
anymore.

The house we sat in, shakes and trembles,
Perhaps the drawers are empty and tarred with
lead
And no love remains, but
the mood can still be enhanced by candlelight.

                    And I shall try to follow through with it.

We sit here presently, crossroads and intersection alike
An interjection, an exclamation, and a lack of
responsible action.
Tell me, have we really come so far from the starting
line?

Eyelids notwithstanding, I see your pithy eyes
Staring into my soul
Have I done wrong by you,
Covering your flaws with my pretender smile?
The rain crashes through the windows,
And almost breaks the glass.

The glass breaks soon enough, as all things, I have
realized, do.
The pieces cannot harm us though
It shall harm us if we let it, the incumbent destroyer.
We are separated in thoughts, but a bridge is still
possible.

 Only, how do we commit to dreams?

We simply let Sarajevo's church bells ring rich and
vibrant
It will keep the evil at bay
And for you, I shall lay to rest my past
I will build a castle from the broken shards of glass
It will withstand the mortar shells.

With my tears, I shall write this older self's eulogy
And rebirth as music found only on Albion's shores
The mood thus, shall finally be enhanced by
candlelight.

Mrs. Doe shall play her cello still, the incumbent
saviour.
 And nothing will remain between us but the river
Rhine
 And it shall be purely and utterly sublime.

Ashes to ashes

Ashes, ashes.
The hungry children of broken brandished
boulevards
They cry at the world's apathy
The bombs keep dropping, breaking the human
spirit, piece by piece
While you, you oil your cars with their tears
You stitch your clothes with the money made,
from rubbles of their memories and dreams.

I heard of one who lost their mother to your silly
game of cat and mouse
And another, that lost their childhood love.
Black tar, whereupon once stood their lovely
house.
Now,
Only ashes and ashes.

You look for your next house to buy
You sign the necessary bonds,
While breaking their "unnecessary" bonds.

With your suit and your silly tie,
You hide behind mountains of bureaucratic paper.
Yes, you play chess,
But only use the pieces of pawns.
Yes, you love chaos
But you love money more.

They go hungry
While you sit in your mansion and sip on the latest tea,
buying the latest cosmetic...
...to hide your demons, I'm assuming?

They cry with no hope.
While you plan out the next rubble.
Waging war under the guise of freedom.
Huh, ironic.
They now have no roof.
Only ashes, and ashes.

And soon, they may die
While you'll keep on living unbothered.
But that's alright.
Even you will have nothing soon.

Because one day,
You will die, too.
Only ashes, and ashes.

The Void

Your heart's an ocean,
That hides the deepest secrets.
Of mysteries unthinkable
And depths unfathomable.

For many a long night
Of wonder and stargazing
Of constellations, of planets
Of systems, of long dead stars
Of galaxies and life, much like ours!
Sleeping, I float away dreaming.
Dreaming, I float away sleeping.

- A love letter to space

Becoming

What's wrong with change?
Nothing inherently, I guess
You're becoming something new.

Hey, it's like a chrysalis!

The future is ahead.
So, take its hand and say,
"I'll soon **be-coming** over there".

It's your crescendo

Swallowed Whole

Little swallow runs up to fly, a hundred
times.
Yet falls down on his face, a thousand times.
Branded "failure" by everyone else, a
saddening conclusion,
His wings were too short, a maddening
situation.

Should've been home by yesterday
Now he is stuck, searching for a way out
While in a world full of robots and
automatons and the modern crazy
One tried hard to overlook their
humanity and fit in.

Tiny Thin Hearts

To be surrounded by all the light of Albion's
shores,
And yet to have no way to find your land
This land that we both grew up in.

Seeing and knowing
Understanding and forgetting.

Can we take a moment to simply walk the shores again
For we may soon not know how to remember
And how to assure ourselves that night does pass into
day
That your wounds do pass into nay.

Into the hardened mountains of your heart
I lay claim to forever pick away
Picking at the hardest of sinews
Like all the gold in Solomon's mines
And I would pick away one more time,
I am your miner, your tiny thin-hearted coward.
I am lost, I am found
And yet I am nowhere to be seen.

And with all of the love in your eyes
 I still find myself hollow.

With all the might of your wicked heart
The day you walk, please do not tear me
asunder.

When I looked through the curtains, I found
Nothing but my own heart enclosed in a glass
enclosure.

I tried to break free, oh, I did
But I could only muster out one, two and
perhaps three.

I am lost, I am found
I am down, I am out
I see none but myself

I am a painter, I am a crutched frail old man
I am thirteen, I am twenty, I am forty, I am ninety
I am yours, but I am not.
I am merely your tiny thin-hearted coward
So, please, forget me,

And do not forgive me.

The 25th Year Of My Life

The 25th year of my life taught me to be alone.
For none but your own will guides the way,
When the light of the stars fail at the break of day
You stand solo, bewildered at the edge of the world.

It has taught me that not all things broken are lost
Not all things mended are whole again
Some coloured lines in the clouds, I see too,
Not silver linings, though, too far and few in between
to be visible.

The year has taught me the value of time
To never be too early nor late for the things that need
be,
Things that once lost can never be found.

The 25th year of my life, one quarter faded
away in the sands of time,
My hearing is lost, I cannot listen anymore,
Cornered into a glass cage with no waves of
sound,

Nor any vibrations of air.

The year has taught me to breathe in the nightly cool
breeze
Alone in my bed, feeling as cold as the grains of the
Sahara sands
Does loneliness affect me?
I cannot tell you; I think it has always been with me.

My eyesight is gone, I cannot see far away
The pikes at steady hand, rays of prickly cacti sun
The centre of the storm forever at my lap
Dozing off to a world where I am deaf and blind.

My mouth still works, however,
So perhaps there is still some more life for me to give
to you.
I do see some semblance of light,
In this everlasting horizon's darkness.

The 25th year of my life
Filled with pain and torment
But now, I have light and guidance again
The light has taught me, too,
Perhaps I am not blind yet.
Nor deaf yet,
Well... I won't be late again.

There and Not

I saw a crowd of pebbles down under,
Illuminating the beaches.
They remind of fireflies on a hot summer's day,
And as the crow flies, the destination is a long ways
away

Where the hard man's toil empowers the fortuitous
concrete jungle, and yet he is revered,
Where the humbleness of the common man will not
entitle the entitled.
And when these facts resonate within the mind
So deep within, they will never tear asunder again.

I am here, then I am not anywhere else,
Your heart in my heart, lovingly entwined.
And maybe we were perfect how we were,
But chose a diversion that led us nowhere.

Or perhaps something tells me there never was a
perfectness,
To think of us as perfectly perfect was the folly
to begin with.
Perhaps the world was meant to be arbitrary,
Nothing exists in the day; nothing subsists in
the night.

Can it be that from the high heavens to nigh
mountains
Everything is cut from the same cloth that we
ourselves bear,
A cloth of the one true ocean that leads us to
haggard realisation.
                    As are you, as is me.

I am here, then I am not there,
But to be here, is to be a thing.
To be a thing is to be grasped
Then to be grasped is to be of
                              mine own.

But the green little hamlet both exists and does not,
The lark both sings and does not,
It is all in the mind, the journey had already begun.
          Where it leads, who knows?

Can it be that pain remains and yet subsides?
The moon does the same, it remains and yet also a part
is lost at once.
Two halves, black and white, both dancing the same
tune,
Both ephemeral and ethereal
What is then real and then what is not?

Can it be that when I am found that I am still lost?

That when I am there, then I am quite not?

This Is Not a Poem for You

On a walk beneath the cliff'd archway formed,
By an err of nature's way,
The red letters of the sunlight at bay
tattoos the skinned knees of yours truly.

The adventure always ends in a trifle
Over the heart's want to both ebb and flow.
The oceanside cliffs, its soil falls down and over under
thoroughly.
The fish and the dirt, the barnacles of the violet turf.

Not many dare to record such instance
Leaning towards a tomorrow that is apparently
arriving,
But never arriving, never consoling.
A moment of grey seagulls' cry
Horsing through an eternal lie
Never arriving...
Never aside me.

Nature's error is nature's gift
Cartwheels of magnets.
The daffodils seldom would dance for a single soul,
The daffodils are collective, they are for all to enjoy

In sacred touch, in battered hue
The cliffside soils do fall upon the fishes
Their infinite encircling endeavour
Everlasting and dizzying.

The archway is nature's error and respite
Its ebb and flow,
Nature makes no errors,
It is all in the mind.

Soon, the fishes do leave,
The cliffside soil that drops into the ocean
Too much to bear after a certain instance.
Their great swimming circles are now but still
waters,
And no seagulls cry foul.

This is the truth,
And the antidote to poisoned vision.
The grey is the light,
The darker the **hue**, the greater my respite.

Indeed, these are not words for you to love,
This is not a poem for you.
But perhaps this is a poem for me,
And I alone will love, as I have loved.

On Trees

Can trees feel?
The pain of being chopped down bit by bit
To be sold off to the market of fate?
When a part of you is lost forever
Away from you, never to be seen again?
 I wonder if trees are lonely
Giving shade to the one and many
Each traveller bringing their own story
But never talking back?

Can trees feel?
The knowledge of losing touch with their fruits?
Nurturing them and sheltering them.
Until it is time for them to leave.
Oh, I do wonder.

And yes, springtime returns with new coating and
new pretty leaves
But does the tree long to see the same leaf again that
it once so loved?
Even while knowing they will never be met again?

Oh, the pain of a heartbreak.
Come forth the pain of a loss
Comfort the want of the soul
Peace be upon all those that left, and all those that
remain...
And my friend, if trees can feel what I feel in times
aplenty,
I shall plant a million more to keep my cold bones
company.

Loss

Yellow sun shines in exuberant display, brightening
your smile, a little more each passing second,
Each passing second...
Ah, to be fortunate enough to spend this time with
no ground underneath me
Only air, only rain.

Your outline seated upon the rocks
Laughing, as you see me tumble down a ladder
The rocks have aged,
I wonder, have you?
Your outline is none but a shape in my memory
now.
And it is a circle,

Nothingness, dark and **opaque.**

There **is** never going be a time like this
Ever again.

Focus on your present and the present will gift
you.

JAHNVI 2019

Departing

I saw you again yesterday
The lines on my face, digging deeper each year since
last we met.
"You look older", you said.
It did not surprise me.
The young smile of a past memory, ageing, finally
catching up with the already aged life that was being
lived earlier.

If you ask me to stay, I would, I think.
Beneath our feet,
the muddy waters of a shoreline at sunset
Our footsteps echo and sync with the seagulls and
their familiar shriek
And the image of my mother, waving from a warm
distance,
laughing at our silly evening chatter.

The wind, too, blows past your ear,
Carrying your essence to some foreign land that I
cannot yet go to.
I do hope you're well, especially without my
naggings
Oh, how I caressed your hair, many sleeps ago.

I would stay, I think.
But my face-lines haven't dug their deepest yet.

The bells ring now, I had best be going.

Trapeze

I'd like to believe I am not very old yet,
Between the fire that burns too bright and the
blackness that seeps in,
I find the most comfort.
For that has been my life, most of my life.
In-between a heaven and an impending abyss.

Between a blue rose that sings
And a mole that digs beneath your feet
Not yet flying, but not yet grounding.
Just like the lads walking on the wires,

      Perhaps I, too, need

            something to latch onto.

The Death of a Man

Confronting a burning desire,
Triumphant and foolhardy, he stands at the
precipice
The man whose might is measured in music
That plays for the common masses.

In his passing, we feel the energised mettle
To keep one foot forward over the 'morrow.
And lead, with the growing urge to dream.
A nightly solemn sonnet ever on the mean.

The character of the mighty, the truly mighty
Will not ever be broken.
In his passing, the embrace of night remains cold.
The darkness also weeps, and the morn' still remains
asleep

But the teaching of virtue
And the ringing of bells that ring for passing,
It rang once beyond the river and fell flat.
For the ringing on that day akin,
and ably comparable to the beating of angel's
wings.

In the passing of a great man whose courage lay bold,
Shall we beat the marching of drums.
His passing is understood as the dusty roads of day,
glides down into nightly embrace.

The kinsfolk he leaves behind,
And the dreams they nurtured,
Find their fulfilment now, without his arms to hold
fast,
As once they had done, years and years inside
memory's coves.

The death of a man is not easy,
But if held true to his character,
Even today, in passing, the war drums sound,
And the eagles on free wings soar.

The Discoverer of Life

On his way to discover a shrewd thing called life,
He first discovered pain. It hurt.
The skin off his bare back eroded to reveal the weight
of the world he was born to carry.
At least, that is what they taught him while he was kept
away from the truth.
The story was not too complex, but rather marred by
characters not too aiding.
That was what led to the tears.
And that exactly is 'pain', my dear.

He then discovered loneliness. It was confusing.
The barren muscles off his aching back mended itself
on the third bell of the clergyman's iron hand.
It seemed like bliss.

But then his back mended itself too tight and
where there was supposed to be life,
there remained only stone.

A stony back, for the stony soul
Black stones on his rocky, fearful heart.
And that exactly is 'loneliness'.

He then discovered envy.
It was suffocating.
One, two, three, the bells rang again
But they dissuaded him not.
They aware'd him not.

He was sat between the gratitude of his life
And the vast distance that separated the
destination he wanted to reach.
And it was staggering.
In the end, the deserts of this distance
Lent him no water on his journey.
Merely the dirt found on the yellow road
And the orange suffocating sky.
And that exactly is "envy", sweet child.

He then discovered betrayal.
The boat of hardened trust,
Broken by harder rust.

The rusty spiked demons of mine own nightmares
surrounded him,
and left him nothing but a flooded ledge.

The demons laughed as they saw him struggling to
survive a leaking boat
In an ocean of shark-infested water, somewhere
between Atlantis and Hollowman's cove.
And that exactly is betrayal, left with no hope

Or so they would think.

He swerved and slipped through
Finally discovering hope.
Soon it was realised that the boat is not hollow
Your hands in the form of mermaid's songs
Mend the leaks.

The mermaid sirens sound bold
And alluring.
Drawing upon some distant foggy appearance.
And in coloured vision,
the notes of the siren song nudge him closer.

It is the forgiving tune.
Fairly, as was always his love for you.

When she lied on these arms, she flew off to lands
and mountains of alpine beauty
 How he'd love to join you there
And sing of fields of green
In your favourite houses and towns

He would love to join you there
That is the one place where he could have you
forever.

One minute away from your smile
Frowns the heart to blackened guile
The heart shall then always want your smile
Brightening, and ever-magnifying.

Hope was found thus, in a heart not of his own
But it was his own, that he unselfishly loaned.
And then, everything was learnt.

Everything he saw, everything he'd come to know.
The discoverer finally had discovered life.
And if I were a betting man, I would gamble
you're just like the discoverer, aren't you?

The discovery has been tough but sweet.
Wouldn't you agree?
Come on, don't be shy.

This man's hope was of legends.
And on the 'morrow, shall he hope again.
And so shall you, no?

A Call to the Ancestral Land

The water in mine hand
Flowing on from hills and which, from other hills,
from the mighty Siang
The bones of Abutani still call out.
Nothing so ever really dies.

The green valleys of dema-ji; obonori's waters
encompass the oddly beautiful
In folly mighty, in green, emerald beauty
 In hunting heart within, in striking obsidian
rhythm
All has one true goal.

We must away, and must away till
Foe and friend alike, we shall meet again,
In Ui-Among, in Abutani's land.
In another time, in another life,
In heart and soul, in gaia's pale blanket of gold.

(In the Mishing community of Northeast India, Ui-Among
is the spirit world, and Abutani is the first human created
on earth by the spirits.

This Ui-Among takes the form of heaven in this
indigenous culture).

Yummair-Mé:tom (Eventide Ballad)

(This poem is written in the Mishing language, a Tibeto-Burman language of Assam, North-east India)

Ka:begtila dungkang nok mikmodém
 (I see your face still).
 Ngokké manying a:ra:do
 (Inside my dreams)
Du:tíla dungkang nokké doying-kídídé
(Your stories remain still)
 Ngok a:nkéng a:ra:do.
(Inside my heart)

Okolo dupakkang nok aya:dé?
(Where did I lose your love?)
Nok kayumné yírnamdé?
(And your beautiful smile?)

Nok médírsunam miksidé, du:tíkang silosin,
(Your saddened tears, exist today still, and were
left behind)
Ngok a:ra:do asin-tarépé igela
 (As a scratch,
              above my own heart).

Nostalgie

To hold your hands in the same manner I did some 20
years ago; some thirty years thence have passed lost in
your eyes,
And flowed my heart into the same sea
The same one that coloured your eyes so brown.
Brown as the sands of your love.
The same love, I reminisce
The same love, I miss.

If I could live a thousand moments in heaven, I
would rather choose to spend it with you.

But therein lies the beauty!
I would be with you
And I would still be in heaven, in heavenly grace, in
heavenly respite,

Forever, in your memories.

Climb

I have seen hundreds of days pass
And they all reek of the same dastardly cloud,
The smell of failure and the smell of thorns, on the
way to high heavens proud.

Floral garlands adorned from above,
To commemorate even the slightest of fight,
The road ahead is black and the road ahead is steep
But the heart within is red, and the heart within
means might

The vigour with which one stands
And passes through no man's land
The character it builds, the strength it brings into
existence,
Is the person that must be embodied, that is the
firmness in their hand.

The courtyard of broken beautiful shards has
housed many a broken pitiful heart,
The cards of destiny, the tryst with fate
From the mountain peak of "I cannot",
Shovelled to the ground and sculpted into weapons,
into
The will with which one perseveres,
the sword with which one leads again and again.

But no matter dusk, no matter dawn
The impossible climb is but one frogleap afar
A jump with hardened legs,
An act of willful heart and,
Nothing left behind for to regret so,

No left-behinds out of any left-behinds.

Reliquaie

How funny life is,
To have been thrust into a series of suffering and
pain
Without ever having the option to have not been
born.
But as the tadpole grows,
And earns its legs running free,
So, too, must you follow your destiny.

Life is marred with tragedies and sorrows,
And only the truly lucky live to see a better
tomorrow,
But you are not a leaf blowing with no direction
You were meant to be here.

How funny life is, to have been chosen of the
billions of possibilities
To inhabit this blue earth.
Therefore, you owe it to the happenings of chance,
To live and continue this velvety dance.

Oh, to have been left with a soul.
By the Almighty or whatever high power there may
be,
To be soulful is to have the right to fight,
Oh, little one, you worry but know your soul is filled
with might.

And the mightiest have seldom been unafraid,
For fear is the best catalyst of circumstance,
When the devil claims your desire to fight and bet,
Let your heart yell, "not yet, not yet".

The cards you were dealt with, let them be
What matters are the books you yourself choose out of
destiny's shelf,
You were not here to lose to any happenstance.
And certainly, my dear, not to lose to yourself.

Your story hasn't ended, nor has it reached its
crescendo,
And soon, the pain will subside,
For even the tides lose intensity sooner or later, and
the grey soil remains.

And just as you trace the seams of your life,
You will sew a costume worthy of kings
You will weave gold out of the thousands of hurts,
And you will sculpt a heart worthy of the strength
of a hundred lions
And just as your head is left adorned with jewelled
wreaths,
So too, my dear, you must live, you must live.

So that, you and I, we both will stand at the sun's
door,
And when the halos of light ask of us,
"what hath you done in your time below?"
We shall stand, head high, and say,
"We danced at the devil's door, and we lived,

And we lived!"

About the author

T.U. Patir has definitely been accused of writing too much about sadness. But he doesn't budge. Sadness can often be beautiful, he says.

He lives alone (not as much because he wants to, but more so because people can't put up with him) and would love to spend time with his dog more often.

He can **often** be found here: patirwrites99@gmail.com

If you liked this book, then please do review it on the platform you bought it from. It helps a lot!

www.ingramcontent.com/pod-product-compliance
Lightning Source LLC
La Vergne TN
LVHW010820200726

843507LV00003B/653